CATERPILLAR D-2 & R-2
PHOTO ARCHIVE

Bob LaVoie

Iconografix
Photo Archive Series

Iconografix
PO Box 446
Hudson, Wisconsin 54016 USA

© 1999 by Bob LaVoie

Iconografix books are offered at a discount when sold in quantity for promotional use. Businesses or organizations seeking details should write to the Marketing Department, Iconografix, at the above address.

Library of Congress Card Number: 98-75275

ISBN 1-882256-99-9

99 00 01 02 03 04 05 5 4 3 2 1

Printed in the United States of America

Cover and book design by Shawn Glidden
Edited by Dylan Frautschi

PREFACE

The histories of machines and mechanical gadgets are contained in the books, journals, correspondence, and personal papers stored in libraries and archives throughout the world. Written in tens of languages, covering thousands of subjects, the stories are recorded in millions of words.

Words are powerful. Yet, the impact of a single image, a photograph or an illustration, often relates more than dozens of pages of text. Fortunately, many of the libraries and archives that house the words also preserve the images.

In the *Photo Archive Series,* Iconografix reproduces photographs and illustrations selected from public and private collections. The images are chosen to tell a story—to capture the character of their subject. Reproduced as found, they are accompanied by the captions made available by the archive.

The Iconografix *Photo Archive Series* is dedicated to young and old alike, the enthusiast, the collector and anyone who, like us, is fascinated by "things" mechanical.

Iconografix Inc. exists to preserve history through the publication of notable photographic archives and the list of titles under the Iconografix imprint is constantly growing. Transportation enthusiasts should be on the Iconografix mailing list and are invited to write and ask for a catalog, free of charge.

Authors and editors in the field of transportation history are invited to contact the Editorial Department at Iconografix, Inc., PO Box 446, Hudson, WI 54016. We require a minimum of 120 photographs per subject. We prefer subjects narrow in focus, e.g., a specific model, railroad, or racing venue. Photographs must be of high-quality, suited to large format reproduction.

I dedicate this photo archive to the memory of P.A. Letourneau. I thank him for the wonderful images he brought to our attention and his awesome contribution to our hobby.

Caterpillar J series D-2 with Trackson loader clears snow from Hwy. 30 in Valparaiso, IN. Working for the state highway commission on January 23, 1943, in 8 hour shifts, it uses 1.5 gallons of fuel per hour.

INTRODUCTION

With the formation of the Caterpillar Tractor Co. in 1925, the world of track-type power changed forever. In 1931, Caterpillar successfully placed the first practical diesel engine into a crawler tractor and the rest is history. With the fuel economy of the diesel being its strongest selling point, the company went on to slowly remove the gas powered tractors from its line.

One of the last to go was the R-2. This little tractor was extremely popular in the United Kingdom as well as in the USA. A tractor with the same name had been produced earlier in limited numbers for the U.S. government. The 5E or 3 speed R-2 was very similar to a model 22 but was only available in wide gauge. Only 83 units of this version of the R-2 were produced.

The J model or 5 speed R-2, which is covered here, was the gas model of the J model D-2. Two serial number prefixes were issued to this tractor: 4J for narrow or 40" gauge and 6J for wide or 50" gauge. Produced from 1938-1942, production was modest. Only 1,185 4J tractors and 1,150 6J tractors were produced.

At the same time Caterpillar was producing a far more successful crawler. It was the Diesel D-2 tractor. The first series of D-2 was known as the J series. The 3J was the narrow or 40" gauge, and the 5J was the wide or 50" gauge. As production of these models ended, they went on to the U series. In this series the narrow or 40" gauge was the 4U, and the wide or 50" gauge was the 5U.

The D-2 went on to be a very popular tractor. Eventually the 2 cylinder starting engine - or "pony" - gave way to the direct electric starting system and glow plugs. Production ended in 1957, but many D-2 tractors still operate daily in agricultural and hobbyist settings across the country.

Acknowledgments

The photographs which appear in this book were made available by the Caterpillar Inc. Corporate Archives. We are most grateful to Caterpillar Inc.

Special thanks to the Antique Caterpillar Club for their assistance in the preparation of this book. For information on the club or membership inquiries, write to:

International Business Office
10816 Monitor-McKee Road N.E.
Woodburn, OR 97071

Owner E. Toshiuma of Arroyo Grande, CA, uses his D-2 and 3 bottom plow to prepare land for tomatoes in June 1939. Covering 7-8 acres in a 10 hour day, he saves $2.25 per day over his former gas tractor.

Owner E. Lage and Sons of Hood River, OR use the 5J D-2 with seat fuel tank to disc in their cherry orchard on April 16, 1940.

Sheffield Steel Corp. of Kansas City, MO uses its J model D-2 to load trucks with clay in August 1945. This machine, equipped with a Trackson loader and Hyster towing winch, has the longer 5 roller track frames. These were standard on loader tractors along with a solid beam rather than a main spring.

Ernella Orchards of Belvidere, NJ, is using their 5U D-2 with toolbar dozer to pile brush in 1954. The arms of the tool bar can be turned to the back of the tractor to accommodate a ripper.

Martin Scholz of Hillsboro, OR uses his D-2 to pull a John Deere cultivator, harrow, and roller to prepare a field for barley in May 1951. Notice how this tractor is equipped with fender fuel tank, wide pads and a lighting group.

A well equipped 5U works at Claremont, MN, with owner Vern Fate. This machine is sub-soiling with the tool bar arrangement on April 24, 1955.

Herbert Stark of Tigard, OR, uses his 5U with tool bar dozer to dig a trench near a church in April 1954.

A 5J D-2 operates a Robinson air compressor off of its PTO with a 4 man pruning operation for Fred Nierman of Cashmere, WA, on his 50 acre orchard.

A 3J D-2 with full orchard fenders pulls a tandem disc, preparing a seed bed for corn at Berrien Springs, MI.

A 5J pulls a pea loader in July 1946 on a 3000 acre pea farm at Walla Walla, WA.

Clarence Wallace of Selma, OR, uses his 5U with logging accessories to skid logs to the landing. Notice the canopy, solid idlers, engine enclosures and Hyster skidding winch.

A 5U with 2S dozer bunching logs at landing on April 12, 1957.

Factory photo of the rear tool bar as installed on a U model D-2 with front mounted #44 hydraulic unit.

Planting two rows of potatoes near Cohocton, NY, in third gear, covering 1 to 1.8 acres per hour with a 5U model in 1956.

In July 1950, a 5U pulls a PTO driven Fox chopper in a 25 acre field near New Vienna, IA.

Grizzley Cattle Co. of Walden, CO, uses its 5U with 2A bulldozer to clear snow from a path to a straw stack after an April 1955 storm.

Carnegie Steel of Pittsburgh, PA, uses a J model D-2 with Trackson loader to clean bricks and slag from the bottom of an open hearth furnace at the Duquesne plant in January 1946.

A D-2 with tool bar dozer works to construct a 250,000 gallon dam on the Katina farm near Mitubiri, Kenya, British East Africa.

A 5J pulling a LaPlant Choate Carrimor scraper works near Miami, FL in February 1941.

Working 10 hours a day and moving 3 yards per load, the 5J used 1.5 gallons of fuel per hour.

A D-2 5U model equipped with side boom pipe layer outside of factory. This machine was also equipped with the 5 roller undercarriage, solid idlers and a lighting group.

Two D-2 3J tractors pull a John Deere lister in black loam near Nashville, KS, in July 1945.

A D-2 5U with rear winch being used in a well drilling operation in Pennsylvania in 1954.

A 3J D-2 pulls a model 22 road grader maintaining roads in Illinois in late 1940.

A 5J orchard model rear or tail seat, spreads fertilizer near Yuba City, CA. Notice the check breakers or furrow ridge breakers installed on the front of the roller frames.

Equipped with a hydraulic loader, this 5U loads slabs of concrete into single axle trucks. Note the double control valves for the loader and the hard nose installed to protect the pump and hydraulic tank. Loader tractors were usually fitted out with solid idlers, longer track frames and street pads.

A 3J D-2 plows a field in the Wyoming foot hills.

Pulling a John Deere combine in a Nebraska wheat field, a J series D-2 works in 1942.

Two D-2 tractors working tandem in a Minnesota field. The machine on the right is equipped with a fender fuel tank and a PTO, as well as a patent tag on the rear of the seat. The machine on the left has a seat fuel tank.

Lobosco and Son Contractors of Flushing, NY, use their model 5U, affectionately named "Marie", to spread fill for the International Horse Show at Madison Square Gardens in November 1954.

A D-2 fitted out with a Trackson loader moves snow from the Union Pacific Railroad mainline after a blizzard in Sinclair, WY.

Working in Rio de Janiero, Brazil, a 5U with 2A bulldozer and lighting group clears land in October 1954.

Morton Salt Company of Weeks, LA, uses this 5U with 2A bulldozer and Hyster winch 735' below the surface, stockpiling salt.

Evan Tews of Springfield, MN uses his 5U with toolbar bulldozer to pull a 9' Towner offset disk, disking corn stalks. Also notice the rear PTO.

Working in an orange grove in Corona, CA, a D-2 with full orchard fenders pulls a Dyrr offset disk in June 1954.

Sinton Dairy Farm Company of Colorado Springs, CO, uses its 4U with toolbar sub-soiler to work land for future corn planting.

Audrey Durst uses the right angle drive of his 3J's belt pulley unit to power a Bryon Jackson pump near Santa Rosa, CA, in 1953.

A 5U, with owner Bob Lamoreaux at the controls, pulls a John Deere haychopper south of Comstock Park, MI, in 1952. Notice the front mounted #44 hydraulic unit and guard.

Working a peach orchard near Valley Center, CA, a 5U with double rear hydraulic fittings and a fender mounted battery box pulls two 8' harrows for owner Donald Haskell.

Pfister Hybrid Corn Company of El Paso, IL uses two 5J tractors to pull corn pickers in muddy conditions with wooden cleats bolted to the pads.

The master pin is driven into the track link of the first Caterpillar D-2 to be assembled on February 19, 1938.

Norman Eggleston of Salida, CO, ditches near his ranch with a 4U and 2A bulldozer.

Working near Scottsdale, AZ, a 5U, equipped with a battery box and rear light, works in an orange grove in 1948.

A 5J D-2 pulls a sprayer through deep water on an orchard near Sacremento, CA.

Disking on a hillside in Washington, a 3J D-2 works in 1942. Notice the battery box and lighting equipment fitted to this tractor.

A 3J painted OD green pulls an impromptu grader blade in Tunisia.

A 5U equipped with a toolbar dozer and #44 hydraulic unit cuts a slope near a Pennsylvania pond.

Working near Spokane, WA, a 3J D-2 with factory lighting group plows in a wooded area.

A late 5U equipped with a side boom pipelayer sits outside factory buildings. Also notice the solid front idlers, battery box and lighting group. This machine also has a second tag attached to the rear end listing the transmission group number.

The right side view of the 5U pipelayer shows the counter weights and guard installed to protect the front hydraulic pump. Also notice the tow hook located underneath the tractor.

Owner Paul Wetzsteon of Sula, MT skids logs to a landing on a 160 acre tract of Douglas fir and Ponderosa pine.

A J-model D-2 with extended track roller frames works in a drilling operation.

A 5U model prototype high clearance machine for use in nursery work has been fitted with an extra track roller frame, idler and rollers. It is also equipped with a tool bar and #44 hydraulic unit.

A rear view of the 5U high clearance machine reveals the actual change in height from the drawbar to the ground.

Pulling a wheeled logging arch and equipped with front grill guard, bumper, tow hook and skid pan, a 5U skids logs to a landing.

Montz Brothers of Webster, IA, use a 5U equipped with a tool bar dozer, #44 hydraulic unit and hydraulic lines to the rear of the tractor, to pull a skid of tile to a location in a field.

A U model with Bishop type orchard fenders pulls an Atlas Tumblebug. Look closely at the exhaust manifold turned upside down for orchard work.

A line of new 5U D-2 tractors await shipment from Peoria, IL, parked nose to nose with some of the larger tractors of the product line.

A 5U with 2A dozer and lights carries a well drilling machine into an Oklahoma field.

A factory photo shows a 5U D-2 fitted out with solid idlers, 2A bulldozer and #44 hydraulic unit.

A late 5U shown from the rear, right side illustrates the operator's area. Notice the late style font of the decals.

A 5U D-2 side boom shows the length of reach with its boom extended for pipe laying work.

A factory photo of an earlier U-model D-2 showing the older style font of the decals, as well as a good view of the 2-cylinder opposed starting engine.

Caterpillar President, B.C. Heacock, congratulates Jimmy Colean, an 80-year-old Caterpillar veteran. In the background is the new 3J D-2 which was to be announced at the Power Show in Wichata, KS.

On February 19, 1938, the new Caterpillar D-2 tractor is completed, and Elmer Belsley is seen driving it out of the factory in Peoria, IL.

Caterpillar President, B.C. Heacock, watches a young operator climb aboard the new D-2 tractor on display in Peoria, IL, in 1938.

Caterpillar D-2 tractor and trailer hauls pulpwood from woods to yarding area on an operation in South Carolina.

A U model equipped with a #44 hydraulic unit and a Trackson LW2 loader works to load a spreader in this April 1950 photo.

One example of the hundreds of items Caterpillar used to promote its new machines was this cardboard advertising fan featuring the "Diesel Economy" of the D-2, a J model.

Accurately located holes are provided for attaching tractor equipment. See your "Caterpillar" dealer for detailed information.

"Caterpillar" Diesel D2 Tractor

The company printed these two-sided brochures or "spec. sheets" to show a photo of the tractor on the front as well as a complete list of data about the machine on the back.

Specifications of "Caterpillar" Diesel D2 Tractor

CAPACITY:

The following are maximum horsepowers at sea level, and are taken from Nebraska Tractor Test No. 322:

Drawbar horsepower	25.86
Belt horsepower	31.99

The following are observed drawbar pulls as reported in Nebraska Tractor Test No. 322:

Drawbar pull:	
First	5,903
Second	3,798
Third	3,069
Fourth	2,485
Fifth	1,585

The following calculated values for maximum drawbar pull are based on the observed drawbar pull shown above. When slowed down by overload "Caterpillar" engines develop a considerably greater turning effort at the flywheel (torque), which results in greater drawbar pull at reduced travel speed:

Drawbar pull Maximum:	
First	6,680
Second	4,420
Third	3,570
Fourth	2,890
Fifth	1,840

Speeds in M.P.H. at full load governed engine R.P.M.	
First (150 ft./min.)	1.7
Second (220 ft./min.)	2.5
Third (264 ft./min.)	3.0
Fourth (317 ft./min.)	3.6
Fifth (449 ft./min.)	5.1
Reverse (185 ft./min.)	2.1

Engine—four-cycle, water-cooled:	
Fuel	Commercial Diesel Fuels
Number of Cylinders	4
Bore and stroke	3¾"x5"
Piston displacement	221 Cu. In.
R. P. M.—governed at full load	1,525
Piston speed	1,271 F.P.M.
R. P. M. at maximum drawbar pull (point of maximum torque)	1,000
N. A. C. C. horsepower rating for tax purposes	22.5
Lubrication	Force Feed
Crankshaft:	
Number of main bearings	5
Diameter of main bearings	2¾"
Total area main bearing surface	80.3 Sq. In.

Starting Method:

Independent, two cylinder, horizontal opposed, 4-cycle gasoline engine, equipped with high tension magneto, down-draft carburetor and flyball governor. Bore 2¾". Stroke 3". 10 H. P. at 3,000 R. P. M. Drive by multiple disc clutch and helical gears to flywheel.

Length of tracks on ground (center drive sprocket to center front idler)	4'-6½"
Area ground contact (with 12" track shoes)	1,308 Sq. In.
Over-all:	
Length	8'-11⅝"
Height (measured from tip of grouser of standard track shoe to highest point, exclusive of exhaust pipe and air cleaner inlet screen)	4'-9⅜"
Ground Clearance (measured from lower face of standard track shoe)	9"
Height drawbar above ground (measured from lower face of standard track shoe)	12"
Lateral movement drawbar (measured at pin)	20"
Track:	
Width of standard track shoe	12" *
Height of grouser (measured from upper face of standard track shoe)	1⅞"
Diameter of track shoe bolts	7/16"
Diameter of track pins	1⅛"
Diameter of track pin bushings	1 11/16"
Steering	†
Number friction surfaces in each steering clutch	16
Transmission	‡
Capacities:	
Cooling system in U. S. Standard gallons	7¾
Lubricating system:	
Crankcase, in quarts	13
Transmission case, in quarts	10
Final drive case (each), in quarts	4½
Fuel tank, in U. S. Standard gallons	20

	50" Gauge	40" Gauge
Over-all width	5'-5¾"	4'-7¾"
Weight, shipping (approx.)	6,870 lbs.	6,710 lbs.

†Each track controlled by slow speed, heavy duty, dry multiple disc clutch and contracting band brake.

‡Power transmitted through dry type flywheel clutch to selective type change speed gear set.

*Nebraska Test No. 322 was made with 16" track shoes.

CATERPILLAR TRACTOR CO. PEORIA, ILLINOIS
DIESEL ENGINES—TRACTORS—MOTOR GRADERS—EARTHMOVING EQUIPMENT

WEST VIRGINIA TRACTOR & EQUIPMENT CO.

Patrick St. at N.Y.C. Railroad
CHARLESTON, W. VA.

100 Wood Street
CLARKSBURG, W. VA

Back side of D-2 J model spec. sheet. This contained information such as weight, horsepower and general information.

Accurately located holes
are provided for attach-
ing tractor equipment.
See your "Caterpillar"
dealer for detailed information.

"Caterpillar" Diesel D2 Tractor

(SPECIFICATIONS ON OTHER SIDE)

Front of the spec. sheet for the U model D-2.

Reverse of the U series tractor spec. sheet.

Specifications of "Caterpillar" Diesel D2 Tractor

CAPACITY:	
The following are maximum horsepowers at sea level, as established by manufacturers' tests:	
Drawbar horsepower	32
Belt horsepower	38
The following are rated speed drawbar pulls, observed during manufacturers tests:	
Drawbar pull:	
First	6,250
Second	4,700
Third	3,800
Fourth	3,070
Fifth	1,960
The following calculated values for maximum drawbar pull are based on the observed drawbar pull shown above. When slowed down by overload "Caterpillar" engines develop a considerably greater turning effort at the flywheel (torque), which results in greater drawbar pull at reduced travel speed:	
Drawbar pull Maximum:	
First	6,680
Second	5,470
Third	4,420
Fourth	3,570
Fifth	2,280
Speeds in M.P.H. at full load governed engine R.P.M.	
First (150 ft./min.)	1.7
Second (220 ft./min.)	2.5
Third (264 ft./min.)	3.0
Fourth (317 ft./min.)	3.6
Fifth (449 ft./min.)	5.1
Reverse (185 ft./min.)	2.1
Engine—four-cycle, water-cooled:	
Fuel	Commercial Diesel Fuels
Number of Cylinders	4
Bore and stroke	4"x5"
Piston displacement	252 Cu. In.
R. P. M.—governed at full load	1,525
Piston speed	1,271 F.P.M.
R. P. M. at maximum drawbar pull (point of maximum torque)	1,000
N. A. C. C. horsepower rating for tax purposes	25.6
Lubrication	Force Feed
Crankshaft:	
Number of main bearings	5
Diameter of main bearings	2¾"
Total area main bearing surface	87.9 Sq In.

Starting Method:

Independent, two cylinder, horizontal opposed, 4-cycle gasoline engine, equipped with high tension magneto, down-draft carburetor and flyball governor. Bore 2¾". Stroke 3". 10 H. P. at 3,000 R. P. M. Drive by multiple disc clutch and helical gears to flywheel.

Length of tracks on ground (center drive sprocket to center front idler)	4'-6½"
Area ground contact (with 12" track shoes)	1,308 Sq. In.
Over-all:	
Length	8'-11⅝"
Height (measured from tip of grouser of standard track shoe to highest point, exclusive of exhaust pipe and air cleaner inlet screen)	4'-9⅜"
Ground Clearance (measured from lower face of standard track shoe)	9"
Height drawbar above ground (measured from lower face of standard track shoe)	12"
Lateral movement drawbar (measured at pin)	20"
Track:	
Width of standard track shoe	12"
Height of grouser (measured from upper face of standard track shoe)	1⅞"
Diameter of track shoe bolts	7/16"
Diameter of track pins	1⅛"
Diameter of track pin bushings	1 11/16"
Steering	†
Number friction surfaces in each steering clutch	16
Transmission	‡
Capacities:	
Cooling system in U. S. Standard gallons	7¾
Lubricating system:	
Crankcase, in quarts	15
Transmission case, in quarts	8
Final drive case (each), in quarts	4
Fuel tank, in U. S. Standard gallons	20

	50" Gauge	40" Gauge
Over-all width	5'-5¾"	4'-7¾"
Weight, shipping (approx.)	6,870 lbs.	6,710 lbs.

†Each track controlled by slow speed, heavy duty, dry multiple disc clutch and contracting band brake.

‡Power transmitted through dry type flywheel clutch to selective type change speed gear set.

CATERPILLAR TRACTOR CO. PEORIA, ILLINOIS
DIESEL ENGINES—TRACTORS—MOTOR GRADERS—EARTHMOVING EQUIPMENT

TREANOR EQUIPMENT COMPANY

721 East Main Street
Visalia, California

155 West Inyo Street
Tulare, California

130 S. Main Street
Porterville, California

511 High Street
Delano, California

CATERPILLAR
SERVICE
MAGAZINE

VOLUME 23 — No. 6   APRIL 28, 1954

New D2 Tractor 24

INCREASED horsepower, greater stability, increased operator comfort and easier servicing are a few of the improvements to the new, longer D2 Tractor.

Greater stability has been made possible by an increase in track-to-ground contact area of 6⅛". The increased length was gained in the flywheel clutch compartment between the rear face of the flywheel housing and the forward end of the transmission. The longer clutch compartment moves the engine forward and results in better weight distribution throughout

the tractor. The over-all weight of the tractor was increased 525 pounds.

Through the redesign of the clutch compartment, the flywheel clutch assembly has become much more accessible. The clutch is now access'' le for repair or removal by removing only the starting engine flywheel and the top cover of the clutch compartment (Figure 1).

(Continued on Next Page)

Front cover of the Caterpillar Service Magazine for April 28, 1954, introducing the New D-2 Tractor. This machine had increased power and other service friendly changes like a "split deck" for changing the master clutch without removing the engine.

NEW D2 TRACTOR, continued

The transmission shaft connects to the clutch shaft by means of a split collar coupling similar to that used on the D4 Tractor, making clutch removal easier (Figure 2).

Several changes were made to the track components. The track assemblies are longer, two links having been added to make a 32 link chain.

FIGURE 1—*Flywheel clutch is now accessible by removing only the starting engine flywheel and top cover of the clutch compartment.*

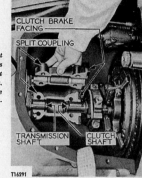

FIGURE 2—*Split coupling connects transmission shaft and clutch shaft. Note clutch brake facings on coupling.*

Roller frames on the new D2 Tractor are longer. The four rollers on each frame are spaced farther apart than formerly. Track carrier rollers, formerly offered as an attachment on earlier D2 Tractors, are now standard equipment on the improved D2 Tractor (Figure 3). Track recoil springs with 25% greater loading are used. Assembled length of the new recoil spring, is $17\frac{1}{16}''$ as shown in Figure 3.

Track adjustment on all D2 Tractors equipped with track carrier rollers is correct when the track can be raised from $1\frac{1}{2}''$ to 2'' above the track carrier roller as shown in Figure 4. Also, as shown in Figure 3, there is $3\frac{1}{2}''$ of track adjustment available on this tractor, as on earlier D2 Tractors.

Improved operator comfort results from a new seat and cushion assembly and more accessible operating control levers.

The seat has been raised 4'' and moved forward 4'' for better operator visibility. Also, where formerly only the back cushions were adjustable, the entire seat assembly is now adjustable. The seat may be adjusted to various positions away from or toward the controls by means of holes in the fender and seat bracket (Figure 5). The seat can be adjusted in increments

of $1\frac{1}{2}''$ and, as adjustments are made to the seat, adjustments must also be made to the fuel tank piping by assembling various lengths of pipe nipple as shown in Figure 6. In Figure 6, the seat is at its extreme forward position.

The capacity of the Diesel engine seat-type fuel tank has been increased from 19 to 26 gallons. Additionally, to keep the cap, the top of the tank, and the seat more clean, the vent and air filter have been removed from the fuel tank cap. Also, a new air filter is used which is located on the bottom of the tank as shown in Figure 6. The new filter is of the self-cleaning type.

(Continued on Next Page)

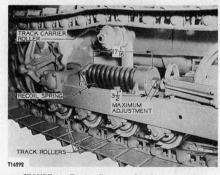

FIGURE 3 — *Track rollers spaced farther apart and a track carrier roller mounted on longer roller frames are standard equipment on new D2 Tractors.*

83

NEW D2 TRACTOR, *continued*

☆

FIGURE 4 —
Track adjustment is correct when track can be raised from 1½" to 2" above track carrier roller.

☆

T16293

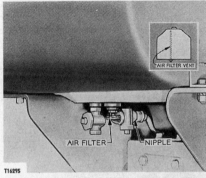

T16295

FIGURE 6 — *Fuel tank air filter and vent are located on the bottom of the tank. When seat is adjusted, longer or shorter pipe nipples are required in fuel line.*

The tool box is now located under the seat cushion in a position similar to the tool box on later D4 Tractors.

A relocated flywheel clutch control lever with improved bearings and redesigned linkage between the control lever and engaging collar is now used. The internal adjustments, however, remain the same.

The steering clutch control levers and linkage have also been changed, and new bumper springs and adjustable lever stops are now used. Steering clutch adjustment on the new D2 Tractor is correct when the steering clutch levers have 1⅜" free movement as shown in Figure 7. This free movement reduces as the clutch facings wear and adjustment becomes necessary. (Steering clutch lever free movement on D2 Tractors with serial numbers prior to 4U6373 and 5U13237 is still 3" from the free forward position.)

Greater operator comfort is now provided by a new steering clutch lever adjustment. A rear stop for each steering clutch control lever limits the travel when the lever is pulled back from the free forward position (Figure 8). The lever movement is controlled by a capscrew, similar to that on the D4 Tractor. The clearance between the end of the capscrew and the stop *should not* be decreased to less than ⁷⁄₁₆" when

(Continued on Next Page)

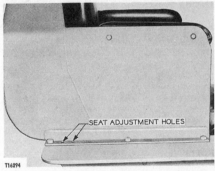

T16294

FIGURE 5 — *For operator comfort entire seat assembly is adjustable to various positions.*

☆

FIGURE 7 —
Steering clutch control levers should have 1⅜" free movement at top of handles for correct steering clutch adjustment.

☆

T16296

NEW D2 TRACTOR, continued

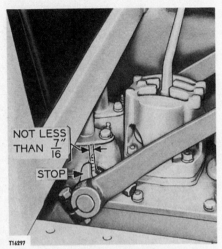

NOT LESS THAN $\frac{7}{16}''$

STOP

T16297

FIGURE 8—*Steering clutch lever stop clearance should be $\frac{7}{16}''$. Stop clearance less than $\frac{7}{16}''$ will prevent proper clutch disengagement.*

☆

FIGURE 9 — *Instrument gauges are now located in an instrument panel.*

☆

INSTRUMENT PANEL

T16298

the control lever is in the free forward position, as this will prevent proper clutch disengagement (Figure 8).

Other changes to the new, longer D2 Tractor provide $\frac{3}{8}''$ thick steel plate fenders similar to those used on the D4 Tractor. The fenders are now formed to provide increased strength.

Longer brake pedals provide greater operator comfort and require less operator effort.

The instrument gauges have been removed from the dash and are now located in an instrument panel which is mounted on the dash as shown in Figure 9. Knock-out holes are provided in the instrument panel for additional instruments and/or switches which may be required.

Few changes were made to the Diesel engine other than moving it forward $6\frac{1}{8}''$. However, the rack setting on D2 Tractors 4U6373 and up and 5U13237 and up has been increased to 1.480″ using the 5F9068 Arm and 5F9071 Block. When making the rack setting with the 3H1690 Gauge, the rack setting is .365″. The in-

creased rack setting increases the drawbar horsepower of the new D2 Tractor to 35 horsepower, and belt horsepower is increased to 42. Engine full load speed remains at 1525 rpm.

When installing 5F9650, 5F9928 and 5F9811 Bulldozer Arrangements on the new, longer D2 Tractor, it is necessary to modify the support plate included in the arrangement. A special instruction sheet, Form No. 31088, is available upon request. All Parts Department stocks of these bulldozer arrangements have been reworked and are directly adaptable to the new D2 Tractor.

48 HP (Flywheel)

Spec. sheet issued in April 1957 showing the late model U series tractor with 48 flywheel h.p. and 38 at the drawbar.

Reverse side of late U model D-2 spec. sheet.

D 2 DIESEL TRACTOR

HORSEPOWER:

Rated at sea level

Drawbar 38
Belt 43
Flywheel 48

Travel Speeds At Rated Engine RPM		Standard Transmission Gear Forward	Drawbar Pull (lb.)	
MPH	FPM		Rated	Maximum
1.8	158	1	7,250	8,120
2.7	238	2	5,200	5,820
3.2	282	3	4,220	4,730
3.9	343	4	3,430	3,840
5.5	484	5	2,230	2,500
		Reverse		
2.2	194	1	6,340	7,100

Tested at Nebraska, Official Tractor Test No. 553
Maximum available pull will depend on traction and weight of the fully equipped Tractor.

ENGINE:

Four-cycle, valve-in-head, CAT* Diesel
Number of cylinders........................ 4
Bore and stroke........................ 4" x 5"
Piston displacement.................. 252 cu. in.
RPM—governed at full load.............. 1,650
RPM—at maximum drawbar pull (point of
    maximum torque) 1,000
N.A.C.C. horsepower rating for tax purposes. 25.6
Lubrication (Full-flow filtering).....Full Pressure
Crankshaft .... "Hi-Electro" hardened
Bearings...................... 5 main bearings
                    aluminum alloy, precision-type
Fuel injection system............Caterpillar-built

FUEL: Burns No. 2 Fuel Oil (ASTM Specification D396-48T), often called No. 2 furnace or burner oil, with a minimum cetane rating of 35. Expensive, premium-quality Diesel Fuel can be used but is **not** required.

STARTING METHOD: Independent two-cylinder, four-cycle gasoline engine. Cooling system integral with diesel engine. 24-volt electric starting optional.

TRACK:

Number of shoes (each side)................ 32
Width of standard track shoe................ 12"
Height of grouser (measured from ground
    face of standard track shoe)............ 1⅞"
Length of tracks on ground (center drive
    sprocket to center front idler)........... 5' 1³⁄₁₆"
Area ground contact with 12" track
    shoes .... 1,460 sq. in.

STEERING: Each track controlled by slow speed, heavy-duty, dry, multiple disc clutch and contracting brake band

Clutch friction material........Woven asbestos
Number of friction surfaces in each
    steering clutch 16

TRANSMISSION: Power transmitted through dry flywheel clutch to selective type speed change. Oil-type clutch optional.

CAPACITIES: U. S. Gal.

Cooling system 7½
Fuel tank 26
Lubrication system   Quarts
    Crankcase 14
    Transmission 8
    Final drive (each)..................... 4½

GENERAL DIMENSIONS:

Length (over-all) .... 8' 11⅞"
Height (measured from tip of grouser of
    standard track shoe to highest point,
    exclusive of exhaust pipe and precleaner) 5' 1⅞"
Width (over-all)
    50" gauge .... 5' 5¾"
    40" gauge .... 4' 7¾"
Ground clearance (measured from ground
    face of standard track shoe to lowest
    point on auxiliary spring shackles)........ 9"
Height drawbar above ground (measured
    from ground face of standard track shoe) 12½"
Lateral movement drawbar (measured at pin) 20"

WEIGHT:

Shipping, (approx.)
    50" gauge .... 7,540 lb.
    40" gauge .... 7,340 lb.
Operating, (approx.)
    50" gauge .... 7,750 lb.
    40" gauge .... 7,550 lb.

CATERPILLAR TRACTOR CO.
PEORIA, ILLINOIS, U.S.A.

CATERPILLAR*

*Caterpillar and Cat are Registered Trademarks
of Caterpillar Tractor Co.

Diesel Engines ● Tractors ● Motor Graders
Earthmoving Equipment

Materials and specifications are subject to change without notice.

FORM 1823—243-E (4-57)   PRINTED IN U.S.A.

CATERPILLAR D2 MODEL TABLE

SERIAL #	START	END	FLY H.P.	FEATURE IMPROVEMENTS
3J1	1938	1947	38	40" Gauge, D3400, 3.75 x 5 – 4 Cyl.
5J1	1938	1947	38	50" Gauge, D3400, 3.75 x 5 – 4 Cyl.
4U1	1947	1957	41	40" Gauge, D311, 4 x 5 – 4 Cyl.
4U5010			48	H. P. Increase
4U6373				One Carrier Roller
4U6655			48	H. P. Increase, Drawbar H.P. – 38
4U7020				Oil Clutch Optional
5U1	1947	1957	41	50"Gauge, D311, 4 x 5 – 4 Cyl.
5U9814			48	H. P. Increase
5U13237				One Carrier Roller
5U14551			48	H. P. Increase, Drawbar H.P. – 38
5U16128				Oil Clutch Optional

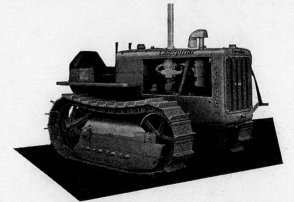
A Caterpillar advertisement announcing the R-2 that can be used with a 3-4 bottom plow.

Working in 500 acres of citrus and avocados near Rancho Sante Fe, CA, an R-2 6J series with Bishop orchard fenders pulls a disk in August 1939.

A factory photo of a 4J R-2 showing the early decal style and placement.

Covering 1 acre per hour, this 6J R-2 plows 8-9" deep in muck near Saranac, MI, in September 1940.

In May 1939, near Tacoma, WA, this 4J R-2 pulls a 6' disk, an 8' spike foot harrow and a Meeker harrow, preparing a seed bed for sweet corn. The tractor works 10 hours a day on 2.2 gallons of fuel an hour.

Owner H.G. Comstock of Santa Rosa, CA, uses his 6J with Killefer 6' disk to farm about 200 acres. Owner claims a fuel savings of $1.40 per day over previous tractor.

Working near Grant, MI, in 1939, this 6J R-2 pulls a 10' disk through an onion field.

Owner Bill Mantai of Watervliet, MI, uses his 4J R-2 tractor to spray 35 gpm in his dormant orchard.

River View Farms of Hamilton, MI, uses its 6J with wide pads to haul celery from the field to the packing shed. Notice the horizontally louvered side curtains on engine sides and the factory canopy.

Working at the Sarasota Airport, Manatee County Highway Commission District #2 uses a 6J R-2 and # 22 blade grader to clear overburden for construction on a new runway.

Joe Priola of Henderson, CO, uses his R-2 tractor to pull a ground driven manure spreader on his large cattle ranching operation in March 1939.

A 4J R-2 tractor pulling 3-bottom 14" John Deere plow in 4th gear at 3.6 mph, plowing about 14 acres in 10 hours near Peoria, IL.

Working near Gary, IN, a 4J cultivates pepper plants on a 100 acre truck farm in low, wet and sandy land.

Wadsworth and Wadsworth of Farmington, CT, uses the power take off on its 4J to power a 400 gallon sprayer in 126 acres of orchard.

A factory photo of 6J R-2 taken for promotional purposes.

Rear view of operator's area of 6J series tractor. Notice decal placement on fuel tank and seat back.

Front view of 4J R-2 outside of Peoria Plant shortly after its introduction.

Left side view of a J-series R-2 engine showing the Eisemann CM4 magneto.

Working at North Port, MI, a 6J pulls a John Deere 10' foot disk, covering 25 acres per 8 hour day. Notice the Bishop fenders and louvered engine side curtains.

A 6J R-2 pulls a number 2 Terracer building a dam near Columbus, GA in June 1939.

Skidding 300 board foot of logs on a 1/4 mile up-hill haul, this tractor handles 8,000' per 8 hour day on 11 cents of fuel an hour.

Optional rear crank starting device used on machines with front mounted equipment. This is tractor serial number 4J786SP. Notice the word "Caterpillar" cast in each track pad.

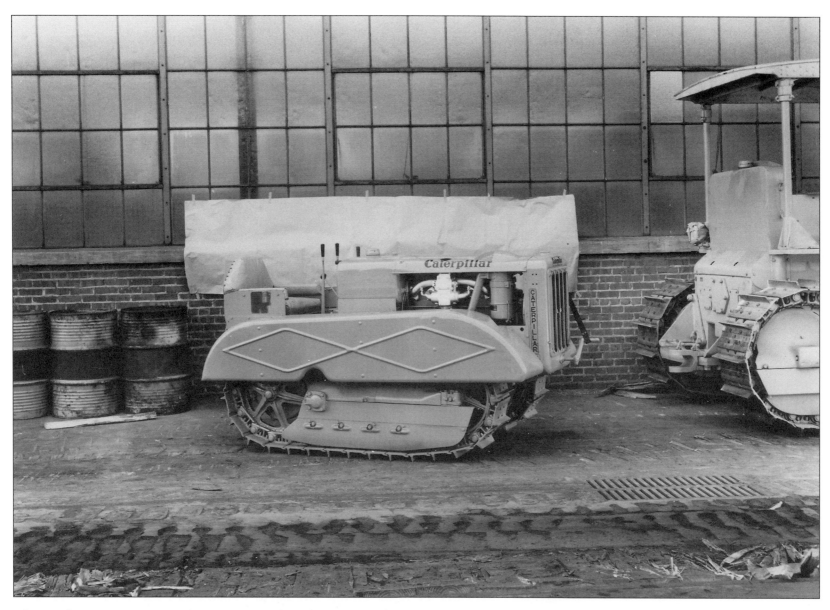

Photo day at a Peoria plant. An orchard equipped R-2 takes its place in line for a publicity photo.

Side view of a 4J R-2 in like-new condition. Notice how the track shields are nearly identical to the D-2.

Owner Walter Luech and his dog, of Trenton, NE, pull a 9' disk tiller and a Miller-basin dammer in 3rd and 4th gear. Also notice the belt pulley stationary drive unit.

A.G. Alan of Richmond, VA, uses his 4J R-2 with LaPlant Choate dozer to clear a site for a service station. The blade is hydraulically controlled by a rear-mounted pump.

Operating a field mill at Lancaster, PA, LeRoy Andrews uses his belt pulley equipped 4J in November 1940.

Farming 480 acres in Seward, KS, G.R. Hicks works his R-2 10 hours a day pulling a 10' tandem disk cultivating corn.

Posed outside of a Peoria factory building, a new 4J R-2 is ready for shipment on the railroad line.

A wide gauge, wide pad R-2 pulls stumps near Jenison, MI, for owner Edward Tanis, preparing land to grow onions.

An orchard equipped R-2 is shown in this factory photo. Notice the air cleaner cover attached to the hood and the fully enclosed fenders.

Frank Tanaka of Gering, NE, pulls a 2-way plow and spike tooth harrow in April 1940.

Working on his farm at Westville, IN, Vernon Forbes pulls a John Deere 3-bottom plow, working 8 hours a day, covering about 14 acres. This tractor is outfitted with a lighting group and rear PTO.

A 4J works 10 to 12 hours a day pulling a combine in a soft, muddy wheat field near Sedgwick, KS, in July 1939.

In April 1940, a 6J R-2 pulls a Rome plow near Atlanta, GA. Covering 1 1/2 acres per hour and working a 10 hour day, it uses 9.5 cents of fuel per hour.

Factory photo of 6J R-2 shown outside of a Peoria plant. This photo shows the color scheme on the front radiator screen as well as decal placement and detailing.

Front of the spec. sheet for the four-wheel drive, rubber tired DW2. This machine was a special application tractor produced in Canada by Crothers Manufacturing.

DW2   RUBBER TIRED DIESEL TRACTOR

HORSEPOWER:

Rated at sea level
Flywheel 50

OPERATING PERFORMANCE DATA:

Travel Speeds at Rated Engine RPM MPH	Transmission Gear Forward	Rimpull (lb.)
3.1	1	7,540
4.7	2	5,680
6.1	3	3,250
8.1	4	2,800
10.4	5	2,250
	Reverse	
4.4	1	6,300

Maximum available pull will depend on traction and weight of the fully equipped Tractor.

ENGINE:

Four-cycle, valve-in-head, CAT° Diesel
Number of cylinders 4
Bore and stroke .... 4" x 5"
Piston displacement .... 252 cu. in.
RPM — governed at full load 1,750
N.A.C.C. horsepower rating for tax purposes 25.6
Lubrication (Full-flow filtering) ...... Full pressure
Crankshaft .... "Hi-Electro" hardened
Bearings .... 5 main bearings
   aluminum alloy, precision-type
Fuel injection system .... Caterpillar-built

FUEL: Burns No. 2 Fuel Oil (ASTM Specification D396-48T), often called No. 2 furnace or burner oil, with a minimum cetane rating of 35. Expensive, premium-quality Diesel Fuel can be used but is not required.

STARTING METHOD: In the seat starting of independent two cylinder, four-cycle gasoline engine. Cooling system integral with diesel engine. 24-volt electric starting optional.

TRANSMISSION: Power transmitted through oil-type flywheel clutch to selective type speed change. Oil-type clutch is optional.

WHEEL DRIVE: Four wheel, tandem drive RC140 roller chain running in oil within sealed chain case.

STEERING: Each chain drive controlled by slow speed, heavy-duty, dry, multiple disc clutch and contracting brake band.

Clutch friction material .... Woven asbestos
Number of friction surfaces in each
   steering clutch 16

TIRES: 14.00 x 20 — 12 ply with non-directional tread. Other treads optional.

CAPACITIES: U.S. Gal.

Cooling system 7½
Fuel tank 26

Lubrication system   Quarts
   Crankcase 14
   Transmission 8
   Final drive (each) 4½

GENERAL DIMENSIONS:

Length (overall) .... 9' 10"
Height (to top of fuel cap) .... 5' 11½"
Width (overall) .... 6' 8"
Wheelbase .... 4' 10⅝"
Wheelgauge .... 5' 4½"
Ground Clearance
   Bottom of chain case .... 15½"
   Lowest point on pan guard .... 17½"
Drawbar height .... 19½"
Lateral movement of drawbar .... 20"

WEIGHT:

Operating (Approx.) .... 8,770 lbs.

Rubber tired conversion manufactured in accordance with CATERPILLAR° design and installation specifications by:

CROTHERS MANUFACTURING LTD.

772 Warden Ave.

Toronto, Canada

°CATERPILLAR and CAT are registered Trademarks
of Caterpillar Tractor Co.

Materials and specifications are subject
to change without notice.

FEB. 1957   PRINTED IN CANADA

Reverse of the DW2 spec. sheet. This machine was a special application tractor produced in Canada by Crothers Manufacturing.

More Titles from Iconografix:

*This product is sold under license from Mack Trucks, Inc. Mack is a registered Trademark of Mack Trucks, Inc. All rights reserved.

All Iconografix books are available from direct mail specialty book dealers and bookstores worldwide, or can be ordered from the publisher. For book trade and distribution information or to add your name to our mailing list contact

Iconografix
PO Box 446
Hudson, Wisconsin, 54016

Telephone: (715) 381-9755
(800) 289-3504 (USA)
Fax: (715) 381-9756

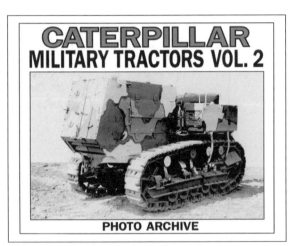

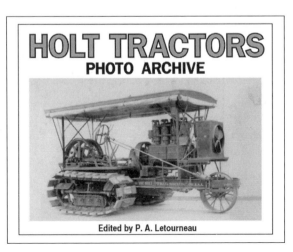

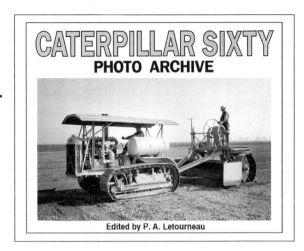

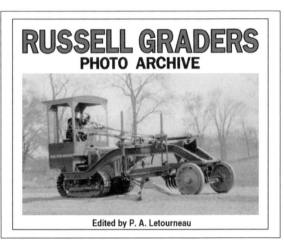

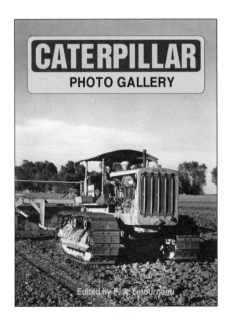

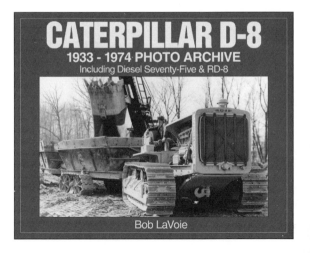